Tiptoe Into
SCARY PLACES

GHOST
CAVES

by E. Merwin

Consultant: Ursula Bielski
Author and Paranormal Researcher
Founder of Chicago Hauntings, Inc.

BEARPORT
PUBLISHING

New York, New York

Credits

Cover, © Alik Mulikov/Fotolia, © martin951/Fotolia, © grahammoore999/Fotolia, © chamnan phanthong/Fotolia, © Santi Rodríguez/Fotolia, © waldorf27/Fotolia, © triocean/Fotolia, and © Ivan Kurmyshov/Fotolia; TOC, © BENVALEE ONTHAWORN/Shutterstock; 4–5, © andreiuc88/Shutterstock, © Lipowski Milan/Shutterstock, and © taviphoto/Shutterstock; 6, © rcimages/iStock; 7, © Jim Plant; 8, © wbritten/iStock; 9, © Albert Russ/Shutterstock and © Ollyy/Shutterstock; 10T, © Susan Law Cain/Shutterstock; 10B, © Roman Zaremba/Dreamstime; 11, © Chrisgel Ryan Cruz/CC BY-NC 4.0; 12–13, © Lipowski Milan/Shutterstock; 14, © Universal History Archive/UIG/Bridgeman Images; 15, © majeczka/Shutterstock; 16, © Sueddeutsche Zeitung Photo/Alamy Stock Photo; 17, © Steve Etherington/PA Images/Alamy Stock Photo and © FocusOnYou/iStock; 18, © Elsa Hoffmann/Shutterstock; 19, © Dave Fahrenwald; 20–21, © John Tu/CC BY-NC 4.0; 21B, © Andrew J Billington/Shutterstock; 23, © tatui suwat/Shutterstock; 24, © Lovely Bird/Shutterstock.

Publisher: Kenn Goin
Editor: Jessica Rudolph
Creative Director: Spencer Brinker
Photo Researcher: Thomas Persano
Cover: Kim Jones

Library of Congress Cataloging-in-Publication Data in process at time of publication (2018)
Library of Congress Control Number: 2017012312
ISBN-13: 978-1-68402-266-3 (library binding)

For more information, write to Bearport Publishing Company, Inc., 45 West 21st Street, Suite 3B, New York, New York 10010. Printed in the United States of America.

10 9 8 7 6 5 4 3 2 1

CONTENTS

Ghost Caves 4

Trapped Forever. 6

Secret of Ben Madigan. 10

A City Below the City. 14

The Shark Man 18

Ghost Caves Around the World 22

Glossary 23

Index 24

Read More 24

Learn More Online. 24

About the Author 24

GHOST CAVES

You enter a dark, spooky cave filled with spiderwebs. Once inside, you slowly walk down a dark, cramped tunnel. Suddenly, you stumble over a half-buried bone. Does it belong to an animal . . . or a human? Then you see movement far off in the beam of your flashlight. Is it a bat—or something **supernatural**?

Get ready to read four chilling tales
about ghost caves. Turn the page . . .
if you have the nerve!

TRAPPED FOREVER

Cades Cove, Tennessee

Deep in the Great Smoky Mountains lies the **valley** of Cades Cove. Locals and visitors have terrifying tales to tell about this area.

Cades Cove

When people take photographs there, mysterious **orbs** often appear in the pictures. And in the darkness of a local cave, a trapped spirit is said to cry out.

The entrance to the haunted cave

In the early 1900s, two boys explored the cave's dark chambers. They entered the cave together, but only one found his way out. The other boy died somewhere within the pitch-black tunnels.

Some say the spirit of the dead boy still haunts the cave. If visitors go deep inside with flashlights, no sound is heard. Yet when they turn the lights off, a distant scream for help pierces the darkness!

Near the cave is a church and an eerie graveyard. Some people have reported seeing ghostly faces in the church's tiny windows.

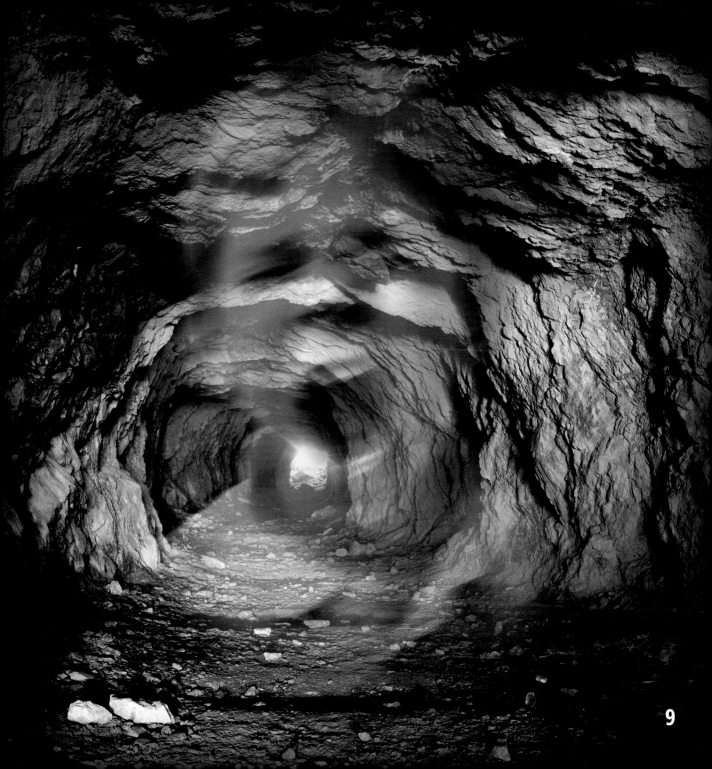

9

Secret of Ben Madigan

Belfast, Ireland

Outside Belfast, the entrance to a cave called Ben Madigan **looms** over green hills. Some say it looks like the eye of an **ogre** staring out at the city.

In 1915, a couple walking by the cave saw the figure of a man hovering above the ground.

The hills outside Belfast

Others who later visited the area reported seeing the same **apparition.**

The mouth of the cave of Ben Madigan

A City Below the City

Under the city of Nottingham, people dug 500 miles (805 km) of tunnels and caves into stone. For almost 2,000 years, the caves provided shelter—and protection from horrors.

In 1665, a deadly **plague** hit England. While people outside died **gruesome** deaths, those who sought safety underground survived.

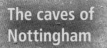
The caves of
Nottingham

Today, visitors report mysterious sights and sounds in the dark passages where many people have lived and died. Some say apparitions appear as darting shadows.

One spirit in the caves wears old-fashioned clothes and cries with grief. Many people also claim to hear the whistle of bombs dropping and distant explosions.

In 1941 during **World War II**, German pilots dropped bombs on Nottingham. The caves protected many people from deadly explosions. Is it the sound of these bombs that can still be heard in the caves today?

THE SHARK MAN

Oahu, Hawaii

Ancient Hawaiians believed in the shape-shifting Shark Man. The creature stood in human form, watching the ocean from Kaneana Cave. When he spotted people swimming, he would dive into the water and turn into a shark.

Once he caught his victim, he returned to the cave with the **cadaver.** After it rotted, the terrifying Shark Man would eat his tasty meal!

Entrance to
Kaneana Cave

Today, people who bravely explore the cave report a bone-chilling drop in temperature. As they crawl through the cramped tunnels, a shadow passes across the beam of their flashlights.

When terrified visitors scramble from the cavern, they sense that they are being followed. One group of explorers who looked back saw a scab-covered figure with burning-red eyes!

Many local people leave offerings of fruit, meat, and rotting fish at the cave. They do this to keep the Shark Man well fed so he won't attack humans!

GHOST CAVES
AROUND THE WORLD

KANEANA CAVE
Oahu, Hawaii

Visit the cave where the hungry Shark Man lives.

THE CAVE OF CADES COVE
Smoky Mountains, Tennessee

Explore dark chambers where a lost spirit wanders.

BEN MADIGAN
Belfast, Ireland

Check out the mouth of a cave that stares like an ogre's eye.

THE CAVES OF NOTTINGHAM
England

Dare to meet the ghostly residents of this underground town.

Arctic Ocean

NORTH AMERICA

EUROPE

ASIA

Atlantic Ocean

Pacific Ocean

AFRICA

Pacific Ocean

SOUTH AMERICA

Indian Ocean

Atlantic Ocean

AUSTRALIA

Southern Ocean

ANTARCTICA

GLOSSARY

apparition (ap-uh-RISH-uhn) a ghost or ghostlike image

burial (BERR-ee-uhl) the placement of dead bodies underground

cadaver (kuh-DAV-ur) a person's dead body

gruesome (GROO-suhm) horrible

looms (LOOMZ) appears over something in a threatening way

ogre (OH-gur) an ugly giant

orbs (AWRBS) glowing spheres

plague (PLAYG) a deadly disease that is spread by fleas and rats

supernatural (soo-pur-NACH-ur-uhl) something unusual that breaks the laws of nature

valley (VAL-ee) an area of low land between two mountains or hills

World War II (WURLD WORE TOO) a worldwide conflict that involved many countries, lasting from 1939 to 1945

INDEX

apparitions 11, 16
Belfast, Ireland 10–11, 12–13
bombs 16
Cades Cove, Tennessee 6–7, 8–9
Nottingham, England 14–15, 16–17

Oahu, Hawaii 18–19, 20–21
plague 14
Shark Man, The 18–19, 20–21
skull 12–13

READ MORE

Black, Sonia W. *The Horror in the Cave (Cold Whispers).* New York: Bearport (2016).

Pike, Christopher. *Spooksville Chilling Collection.* New York: Aladdin (2015).

LEARN MORE ONLINE

To learn more about ghost caves, visit:
www.bearportpublishing.com/Tiptoe

ABOUT THE AUTHOR

E. Merwin writes stories, books, and poems for kids and adults.
Since she began writing about ghosts, mummies, and haunted places
for the Tiptoe series, she has been sleeping with the light on.